Viola Time Runners

T0055794

Viola accompaniment book

Kathy and David Blackwell

Teacher's note

These duet parts are written to accompany the tunes in *Viola Time Runners*. They are an alternative to the piano accompaniments or audio tracks, and are not designed to be used with those items. A separate violin duet book is available providing duet parts for when violas play together with violins using *Fiddle Time Runners*.

Kathy and David Blackwell

OXFORD
UNIVERSITY PRESS

OXFORD
UNIVERSITY PRESS
Great Clarendon Street, Oxford OX2 6DP,
United Kingdom

Oxford University Press is a department of the University of Oxford.
It furthers the University's objective of excellence in research, scholarship,
and education by publishing worldwide. Oxford is a registered trade mark of
Oxford University Press in the UK and in certain other countries

This collection Oxford University Press 2005, 2013, and 2023.

Unless marked otherwise, all pieces are by Kathy and David Blackwell and are
© Oxford University Press. All traditional and composed pieces are
arranged by Kathy and David Blackwell and are © Oxford University Press.
Unauthorized arrangement or photocopying of this copyright material is ILLEGAL

Kathy and David Blackwell have asserted their right under the Copyright,
Designs and Patents Act, 1988, to be identified as the Composers of this Work

Database right Oxford University Press (maker)

Impression: 1

All rights reserved. No part of this publication may be reproduced,
stored in a retrieval system, or transmitted, in any form or by any means,
without the prior permission in writing of Oxford University Press

Permission to perform the works in this anthology in public
(except in the course of divine worship) should normally be obtained from
a local performing right licensing organization, unless the owner or the occupier
of the premises being used already holds a licence from such an organization.
Likewise, permission to make and exploit a recording of these works
should be obtained from a local mechanical copyright licensing organization

Enquiries concerning reproduction outside the scope of the above
should be directed to the Music Rights Department, Oxford University Press, at
music.permissions.uk@oup.com or at the address above

ISBN 978-019-356621-7

Cover illustration by Martin Remphry

Music and text origination Katie Johnston and Julia Bovee
Printed in Great Britain

Contents

1. Start the show 4
2. Banyan tree 5
3. Heat haze 6
4. Medieval tale 7
5. In memory 8
6. Chase in the dark 9
7. Merrily danced the Quaker's wife 10
8. O leave your sheep 11
9. Jingle bells (J. Pierpont) 12
10. Allegretto in C (Mozart) 13
11. The Mallow fling 14
12. Noël (Daquin) 15
13. Finale from the 'Water Music' (Handel) 16
14. Ecossaise in G (Beethoven) 17
15. Viola Time rag 18
16. Busy day (*duet*) 20
17. On the go! 21
18. Blue whale 22
19. Takin' it easy 24
20. Mean street chase 23
21. Ten thousand miles away 28
22. I got those viola blues 26
23. Air in C (J. C. Bach) 27
24. Prelude from 'Te Deum' (Charpentier) 29
25. That's how it goes! 30
26. Flamenco dance 32
27. Somebody's knocking at your door 31
28. The old chariot 33
29. Adam in the garden 34
30. Air (Handel) 36
31. The wee cooper o' Fife 37
32. Aerobics! 38
33. Caribbean sunshine 39

1. Start the show

KB & DB

2. Banyan tree

C string special

Jamaican folk tune

3. Heat haze

KB & DB

4. Medieval tale

5. In memory

C string special

KB & DB

6. Chase in the dark

KB & DB

7. Merrily danced the Quaker's wife

Scottish folk tune

8. O leave your sheep

C string special

French folk tune

9. Jingle bells

J. Pierpont

The introduction is not included in the pupil's book; thus, bar numbers given here follow the numbering in the pupil's book and the D.C. al Fine is written as a D.𝄋 al Fine.

10. Allegretto in C

11. The Mallow fling

Irish folk tune

12. Noël

C string special

Daquin

13. Finale from the 'Water Music'

14. Ecossaise in G

15. Viola Time rag

KB & DB

17
f
mf
21
mp
mp
25
29
mf
mf
33
cresc.
f
cresc.
f

16. Busy day

KB & DB

17. On the go!

KB & DB

18. Blue whale

C string special

KB & DB

19. *Takin' it easy*: next page

20. Mean street chase

C string special

KB & DB

Nos. 19 and 20 are reversed to avoid a page turn.

19. Takin' it easy

KB & DB

Laid-back tempo

21
mf
mp
cresc.
cresc.
26
poco rit.
a tempo
mp
p
31
4
36
mf
mp
41
pizz.
p
pizz.
p
dim.

21. *Ten thousand miles away:* page 28

22. I got those viola blues

KB & DB

No. 21 is shown on page 28 to avoid a page turn in No. 22.

20
mf
f
f
24
rall.
mp
f
mf
mp
f

23. Air in C

Andante
J. C. Bach
mf
mf
6
mp
mp
10
mf cresc.
f
mf cresc.
f

21. Ten thousand miles away

C string special

Sea shanty

24. Prelude from 'Te Deum'

25. That's how it goes!

26. *Flamenco dance:* next page

27. Somebody's knocking at your door

Spiritual

Nos. 26 and 27 are reversed to avoid a page turn.

26. Flamenco dance

28. The old chariot

Sea shanty

29. Adam in the garden

Jamaican folk tune

23
29
f
f
34
mp
mp
39
f
f

30. Air

Handel

31. The wee cooper o' Fife

Scottish folk tune

32. Aerobics!

KB & DB

33. Caribbean sunshine

KB & DB